# *Artistic Feeling and Meditation*

# *Artistic Feeling and Meditation*

Michael Howard

Mercury Press

Cover image from a plaster casting by Michael Howard,
"Turning Point," 2012

ISBN 978-1-957569-06-2



Published by
MERCURY PRESS
an imprint of SteinerBooks
PO Box 58
Hudson, NY 12534
www.steinerbooks.org

# Artistic Feeling and Color Meditations

*"There slumber in every human being faculties by means of which he can acquire for himself a knowledge of higher worlds... Only one question remains—how to set to work to develop such faculties."*

* * *

*"It should be remarked that artistic feeling, when coupled with a quiet introspective nature, forms the best preliminary condition for the development of spiritual faculties."*

Rudolf Steiner, *Knowledge of Higher Worlds*

Meditation can be described in general terms as a way to transform and develop our self. As Rudolf Steiner indicates in the above excerpts, meditation is a way we can develop the inner faculties to perceive and know spiritual realities directly.

The facts and laws of the spirit can be known as a spiritual science in the same way that the facts and laws of the natural world are known as natural science. As natural science depends on developing the capacities of a natural scientist, similarly, spiritual science depends on developing the capacities of a spiritual scientist. For Steiner:

*"Only one question remains—how to set to work to develop such faculties."*

In his many books and lectures—most especially, *Knowledge of Higher Worlds and Its Attainment*, and *Occult Science*--Rudolf Steiner describes these faculties in considerable detail, and outlines numerous ways they can be developed. In this essay our focus will be on the way spiritual faculties can be nurtured through the arts. Our starting point will be to understand what Steiner means by "artistic feeling" in the following context:

*"...artistic feeling, when coupled with a quiet introspective nature, forms the best preliminary condition for the development of spiritual faculties."*

We might easily pass over the term artistic feeling without fully appreciating its meaning and implications for the role of art in meditation and spiritual development in general. Two additional comments by Rudolf Steiner help to clarify his meaning:

> *"A true understanding of the matter cannot be reached if observation of the forms is based solely on intellectual explanation. It is necessary to contemplate the forms with true artistic feeling."*
>
> Rudolf Steiner, October 1907

> *"All the forms do is set the process going that creates the work of art. The work of art is what the soul experiences when it feels the shape of the forms."*
>
> Rudolf Steiner, December 28, 1914
> *Art as Seen in the Light of Mystery Wisdom*

Typically, we think of a work of art as a painting, sculpture or other tangible object. Already in 1914, Rudolf Steiner introduces a radical alternative to this traditional view by suggesting "the work of art is what the soul experiences when it feels the shape of the form"—or the color of a painting, and the melody of the music. There is nothing new in saying works of art affect us deeply, but Rudolf Steiner introduces a new orientation to art in suggesting that the human being is the real and enduring work of art. As an artist uses a paintbrush or chisel to shape a painting or sculpture, the color and form of artworks shape and transform the human soul.

This expanded view of art opens up new horizons in which art can be seen and practiced as a form of meditation and meditation is seen and practiced as a form of art. In this essay we will explore art as a form of meditation through the contemplation of color and form. Special attention will be given to the way we observe color and form as this determines the way color and form live and work within us. We shall see that the full potential of color and form to be worked with meditatively, and thereby to shape and transform us, depends on developing *artistic feeling*.

*What is artistic feeling? How is it developed?*

All artistic mediums—such as color, form, musical sound, human speech and movement— have both physical and non-physical attributes. Like everything in the material world, paintings and sculptures have physical attributes that can be measured or quantified. In addition, all artistic mediums like color and form have non-physical characteristics that cannot be quantified. For this reason, we distinguish between the quantitative and qualitative elements of the sense world.

Our experience of warmth and coolness exemplifies this distinction. On the one hand, we have experiences of physical warmth and coolness that can be measured or quantified with a thermometer. For example, when we meet someone and shake their hand, we may note that their hands are relatively warm or cool. Such warmth could be measured if the person were to hold a thermometer in their hand. At the same time, we might also perceive a certain warmth or coolness in the person's demeanor or radiating from their eyes. It is particularly instructive if we meet someone who has cold hands but radiates inner warmth, or vice versa. Such inner warmth or coolness cannot be measured with a thermometer.

In this example, we use the same terms warmth and coolness to describe two distinct realms of experience—outer warmth/coolness that is physical, and inner warmth/coolness that is not physical. Given our present consciousness we may be inclined to regard physical warmth as real and to explain non-physical warmth as merely the by-product of physical processes. However, for our everyday experience inner warmth is as real as physical warmth. To honor these two distinct realms of experience, we need only adapt our thinking to the notion that reality is multi-dimensional—that physical reality is not the only reality, but simply one dimension of reality.

Even with physical warmth and coolness, we do not necessarily need a thermometer to determine fluctuations in warmth and coolness since our bodies are a kind of thermometer attuned to the rise and fall of the temperature. In a similar way, we can be quite sensitive to other people's inner warmth or coolness. Our ability to perceive the inner life of another person depends in part on our attentiveness to outer perceptions such as facial expressions and body language. In addition, however, we must also be attentive to our own feelings because it is through our feeling nature that we perceive the feelings of others. This capacity to enter into the feelings of others is something of a mystery that warrants pause and wonderment: How is this possible?

If we observe ourselves in the process of observing others, we will notice that more often than not we react with feelings of sympathy or antipathy to varying degrees. Under certain circumstances, however, we may find ourselves setting aside our personal feelings and entering into the feelings of another person. For example, we might be feeling relatively happy, nevertheless, we may be able to feel another person's pain and sorrow. Once we recognize that we have this capacity to live into the inner experience of another as if it were our self, we can choose to cultivate it more consciously.

We can do this by learning to take note of our personal feelings of sympathy and antipathy without dwelling upon them. In doing so, we open ourselves to another dimension of feeling experience, namely, the capacity to feel the subtle and diverse qualities found everywhere in the world. By resisting our predilection to focus on our feeling reaction to things, we open our selves to perceiving nonphysical, or soul spiritual qualities as vividly and objectively as we perceive outer physical qualities.of the world in general.

*Artistic feeling* is the term introduced by Rudolf Steiner to describe the capacity to perceive the qualitative elements in all sense perceptions. With this preliminary understanding of *artistic feeling*, we have a foundation for applying it in meditative and contemplative practice.

## *Contemplating Color*

> *"First we are to concentrate on the color, becoming one with it and allowing it to become us. After identifying with the color as much as possible, we move to an open state of awareness in which an "afterimage" arises."*
>
> Arthur Zajonc, *Meditation as Contemplative Inquiry*, p.102-6

There are at least three distinct realms in which we can contemplate color—the physical realm, the realm of afterimages, and the realm of our imagination. We will begin by observing physical colors, but here too, we have a number of choices to draw upon. Color is a fundamental aspect of the world, and so where possible, we can turn to the colors of nature--the blue of the sky, the yellow of a flower, the green of a meadow or forest, the white of snow—as these colors have a particular vibrancy. Alternatively, we can make our own patches of color using paint, pastels or pencils—creating a 1- 2" circular surface of each color will serve our purpose. As we put the color on a page, we have an opportunity to do so in a quiet reflective mood. Lastly, we can use printed patches of color such as accompany this essay as Figure 1.

In the following steps we will limit ourselves to contemplating the two yellows of Figure 1 but they can be applied to any other colors and color sources.

1. We focus our gaze on the center of the orange yellow patch on the left side of Figure 1 (p 10) for a slow count of 10. Then we move our gaze to a white area on the page where we can expect to see a luminous color

known as the afterimage. We try to attend to this new and different color for as long as possible—typically it will fade within a count of 10. We try to note the exact hue of the afterimage.

2. We follow the same process with the green-yellow on the right: gazing at the center for a count of 10, and then turning our gaze to the white where we should see another afterimage. Again we note the exact hue of this second afterimage. We can go back and forth a few times from the one yellow to the other to help intensify the afterimages and thereby better compare the subtle difference in the color of the two afterimages. If, at first, we see no color but only a luminous patch, we can repeat the exercise over successive days. Sooner or later, we can expect to see a blue-purple afterimage from the orange-yellow, and a red-purple afterimage from the green-yellow.

3. Note that our effort to focus on a physical color for a count of 10 is a simple but real concentration exercise. Likewise, holding our attention on an afterimage color for as long as possible is also a concentration exercise with the added factor that we are learning to focus our attention on something that is more ephemeral, less physical.

4. Next, we set aside the physical patches of color, and with our eyes closed or open as we choose, we try to form a picture or impression in our mind's eye of the two yellow patches. We do not need to spend a lot of time trying to picture each color, just a few seconds calling up the orange-yellow and then a few seconds with the green-yellow. Going back and forth between the two colors every few seconds in our mind's eye strengthens our capacity to visualize each one more vividly.

5. Then we try to form a vivid inner impression of the afterimage colors, that is, the more subtle and luminous blue-purple and red-purple. Again, it can help us visualize these color impressions more vividly if we go back and forth between the two rather than staying longer with one.

6. Next we return to the two physical patches of yellow, and again concentrate on each one for 10 seconds or more, but now in a different way. This time we are not concerned with any afterimages--if we become aware of them at this time, we resist focusing upon them by turning our attention to another dimension of color. As we stare at the two patches of physical color on the physical page, we try to quiet our mind from all distractions—any afterimage, as well as any unrelated thoughts or personal feelings. We only ask our self: What is the quality of this color? Sooner or later, we may notice we are dreaming into the color. The outer duality of the color as separate and outside our self falls away, and instead, we feel ourselves slipping into the color, into a world of yellowness. We do this with the orange-yellow for a few seconds and then with the green-yellow. Once again it helps to move our gaze back and forth as needed from the orange-yellow to the green-yellow as a way to heighten our sensitivity to the different quality of the respective colors. As the feeling of a color becomes more vivid, we can try to dwell in that feeling experience for longer periods.

7. When speaking about the quality of our feeling experience with each color, it is important to reiterate that we are not attending to any personal feelings or associations that may occur to us. If these kinds of feelings arise in

us, it is best to recognize nd honor them in order to then set them aside. In time, we can expect to feel something like a heavy-warmth in the orange-yellow compared to a light-coolness in the green-yellow.

8. Lastly, we take these feeling impressions we had while gazing at the physical colors and call them up in our imagination. Whether we picture the colors or not, the essential thing is to call up the feeling experience—such as the relative warmth or coolness of each color.

The term afterimage is sometimes applied to this last activity of feeling the quality of the color. In the following excerpt, Arthur Zajonc draws attention to the fact that the term 'afterimage' is used to describe two different experiences:

> *"Having fully immersed himself in the yellow, he averts his gaze and allows the nimita or "afterimage" to arise. The nimita is not the complementary physiological afterimage that we all see when we saturate the retina with a color sensation. Buddhaghosa's description makes it clear that the meditant is seeking another kind of afterimage, one that is the interior correlate to the outer impression...Into his open field of awareness there emerges the echo or afterglow of the sense impression."*

By drawing attention to these two meanings, Arthur goes a long way in clarifying the matter. However, I would argue that it would be better to have two different terms. First, having two different words helps avoid any misunderstanding about which kind of experience is meant. More importantly, the term afterimage implies a visual image that suits the luminous complementary color that appears after staring at a physical color. However, when referring to a feeling experience of color, the term afterimage is misleading since no image element is involved. Such a feeling experience is more akin to a musical experience, and for this reason, terms like 'echo' or 'resonance' seem more suitable. It is worth noting that we can feel music resonate within us both as we hear it physically but also after the physical music has ended. Similarly, we can feel the warmth or coolness of a color resonate within us both when we look at a physical color but equally after the physical color is no longer visible. For these reasons, terms like 'color-resonance' and 'form-resonance' seem more suitable for describing the perception of color and form qualities both when they are physically present and when they are not physically present.

In summary, so far we have explored the possibilities of contemplating color in three domains: physical color, afterimage color, and inner or soul color. We have seen how in each domain we meet the challenge of concentrating our attention for a brief period—10 seconds is no small accomplishment. We can work with these exercises primarily as concentration exercises, appreciating that as we extend our powers of concentration from physical colors to afterimage colors, and finally to non-physical color qualities, we extend our powers of concentration to realms beyond the purely physical. Furthermore, in cultivating artistic feeling in order to contemplate the inner qualities of color we have learned to extend our consciousness from the physical to the soul-spiritual in our selves and the world. What begins as an exercise in concentration on an outer or inner image becomes a modest but real form of mediation when we dwell upon the soul spiritual qualities of color.

We will now explore the way artistic feeling can be exercised in contemplating the world of form.

Figure 1

# Artistic Feeling and Two Dimensional Form Meditations

## *Contemplating Two-Dimensional Forms*

In Chapter One we considered how color can be used as the content of contemplation. In Chapter Two we will explore the use of two-dimensional forms as the content of contemplation and meditation.

The following passage from Rudolf Steiner on the form of a triangle offers a starting point for another sequence of contemplative exercises:

> *" I will not only draw a triangle and let it stay as it is, but I will make certain demands on your imagination. You must think to yourself that the sides of the triangle are in continual motion. When they are in motion, then out of the form of the movements there can arise simultaneously a right-angled, or an obtuse-angled triangle, or any other.*
>
> *In this field we can do and also require two different things. We can make it all quite easy; we draw a triangle and have done with it. We know how it looks and we can rest comfortably in our thoughts, for we have got what we want. But we can also take the triangle as a starting-point, and allow each side to move in various directions and at different speeds. In this case it is not quite so easy; we have to carry out movements in our thought. But in this way we really do lay hold of the triangle in its general form; we fail to get there only if we are content with one triangle. The general thought, "triangle" is there if we keep the thought in continual movement, if we make it versatile.."*

Rudolf Steiner, *Human and Cosmic Thought*, Lecture 1
January 20, 1914, Berlin

1. With a ruler and pencil we draw several triangles on a piece of paper as indicated in Figure 2. It is not necessary to make any measurements or technical constructions, but simply make straight lines with a ruler to

draw an equilateral triangle, an isosceles triangle with a narrow base, an isosceles triangle with a broad base, a right-angled triangle, an obtuse angled triangle, and any other possible triangle.

2. Drawing these triangles on paper prepares us to picture such triangles in our minds eye. With our eyes open or closed, we try to picture an equilateral triangle for a moment or two. Then picture an isosceles triangle, followed by a right-angled triangle, and so on. It is no small accomplishment to picture each individual triangle as vividly as possible in our mind's eye for a few seconds.

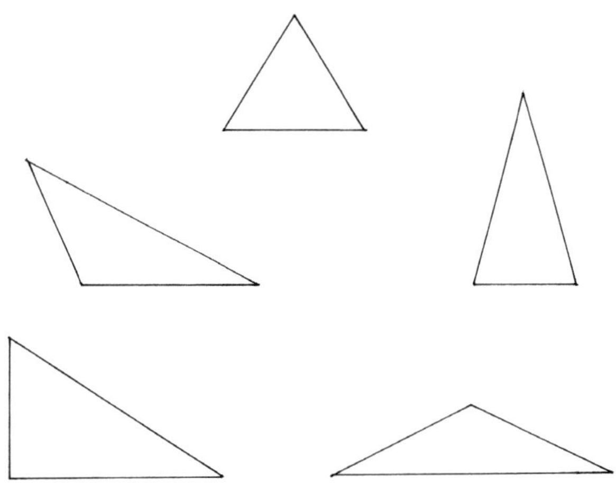

Figure 2

3. Next, we picture once again an equilateral triangle

for a moment, but this time, we picture the base of the equilateral triangle narrowing to create an isosceles triangle that is taller than it is wide. Then, we imagine the base widening so that the isosceles triangle becomes wider than it is tall. Next, we picture the left side of the triangle pivoting until it becomes a right-angled triangle. And then, we allow the sides to pivot further so that the right angle triangle becomes an obtuse angle triangle.

Instead of picturing six separate and fixed triangles we can imagine one triangle transforming into other triangles by picturing the three angles and three sides changing their position and length. Such a moving triangle not only manifests all possible triangles sequentially but all triangles simultaneously if we imagine it moving infinitely fast.

## *From Thinking an Idea to Feeling a Living Archetype*

Arthur Zajonc's description of this triangle exercise suggests a further step:

> *"In this exercise we have moved from a crude sense image (a symbol of a triangle) to a static mental image, to a triangular image in movement, and finally through the flux of individual triangles we leap to the pure thought: triangle...we must reach even beyond triangles in motion to the pure thought: triangle. The thought "triangle" is not dead or fixed, but generative. Thinking and feeling our way into the exercise we realize that the idea of the triangle is the "agent" ("being")...."triangleness."*
>
> Arthur Zajonc, *Meditation as Contemplative Inquiry*, p. 158-61

If asked to picture a form that symbolically represents all triangles, most people would probably think of an equilateral triangle. Picturing a fixed equilateral triangle as a symbolic representation of all triangles is, however, different from imagining a triangle with moving sides and angles that through its very dynamism contains all triangles.

Both the fixed and moving triangles embody the "idea" of a triangle. The difference, however, is that the one is a "fixed idea"and the other is a "dynamic idea.". When we imagine the dynamic form of a moving triangle, we are able to contemplate the attribute or quality shared by all triangles, namely, "triangleness".

When we observe another person we may begin by noting their outer appearance and behavior but we can learn to see through their outer attributes in order to perceive and experience their inner character or quality of being. Similarly, as we take in the great variety of triangles we can awaken to the common quality of all triangles. In this way, "triangleness" is not an intellectual abstraction but a living idea or archetype. We will explore what we mean by a living idea or archetype through another sequence of forms. In the process, we will discover an inner shift in consciousness that marks the transition from contemplation to meditation.

4. We begin by drawing a triangle and circle with some space between them as in Figure 3. Then, we draw two intermediate forms between the triangle and circle as shown in Figure 4. The left intermediate form is more like a triangle but with curved sides, while the right intermediate form is more akin to the circle with only a hint of the three corners and sides of the triangle.

Figure 3

Note: The triangle and circle of Figure 3 are shown in outline in order to reinforce our usual orientation of seeing them as two different geometric forms. When drawing the sequence of four forms shown in Figure 4, do not draw them in outline but experiment with building up a surface of dots or short dashes. Each of the forms is determined by where the dots or dashes form a boundary.

Figure 4

By introducing two intermediate forms between the triangle and circle a new dimension of experience opens up to us. When we see only the circle and triangle, they appear as two distinct forms that have nothing in common with each other. However, as soon as we add the two intermediate forms, it is not difficult to imagine one form transforming into the other. When we see a yellow and blue next to each other they seem to share nothing in common. However, if we place a green, or better still, a yellow green and a blue green, between the yellow and blue we immediately feel how they are related and flow into one another. Similarly, a triangle and a circle have no apparent relationship to each other until we see these intermediate forms. As we can speak of a yellow green and a blue green, I will call our two intermediate forms a roundish triangle and a triangular circle.

Moving from left to right, the triangle that seemed fixed and static begins to expand outward to become the roundish triangle. This expansion extends further into the corners with the triangular circle, and reaches completion with the circle. In going from triangle to circle, the gesture is one of expansion but when we follow the sequence from circle to triangle, we experience an overall contraction. Additionally, as the triangle becomes the circle we note that the forms begin to lift up and become more buoyant. When starting from the circle and moving to the triangle the forms settle down and become progressively grounded.

5. We began by drawing this sequence of four forms as preparation for vividly imagining them. Whether we follow these changing forms outwardly or imagine them inwardly, we are again picturing a moving form rather than a fixed form. Only now, the triangular form changes from an angular form into a curvilinear form—from a triangle into a circle.

When we follow the changing triangles we do so primarily with our thinking. Likewise, it is with our thinking that we note the differences that occur in going from the triangle to the circle. As we follow the changes from triangle to circle through the two intermediate forms, something also begins to stir in our feeling experience. We feel the transformation from triangle to circle as expanding and lifting up. We feel the circle contracting and weighing down as it changes towards the triangle.

Discerning when we are engaged in our thinking and when in our feeling life is not only relevant for the artist but also for the meditant. Towards this end, we will consider yet another variation on a triangle, one, however, that poses a challenge to our conventional idea of a triangle. Arthur points to this:

*"A very particular relationship is expressed in the triangle, which distinguishes it from the circle, square, or any other form. Mathematics is, one could say, all about pure relationships. Everything extraneous is taken away. It is absurd to think of a "roundish" or "squareish" triangle. It would be no triangle at all..."*

6. We draw the construction in Figure 5 as follows:

   i) Lightly mark the very center of the page. About one inch to the left of center, place the point of a compass set at two inches radius and draw a circle around this point A. Place the compass point on the circumference of the first circle at point B, that is about one inch to the right of the center of the page, and draw the circle. This should create two circles that intersect in two places, point C at the top and point D at the bottom as shown in Figure 5. Note that points ABC and ABD are each equidistant from each other.

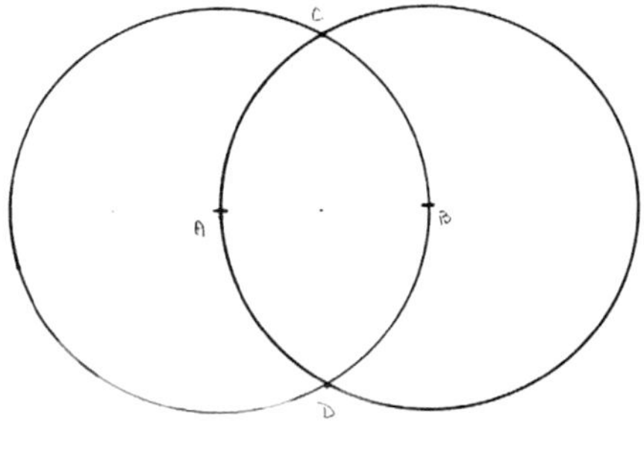


Figure 5

ii) Place the compass point on the upper intersecting point C and draw a circle that should pass through the center points A and B. Note that points ABC can be connected by three straight lines to form the straight-sided triangle ABC. In addition, the intersection of the three circles at A, B and C creates a form that is three-sided but with curved sides. I will call it a "convex triangle."

iii) Now place the point of the compass on point D and draw a circle. Follow this with two more circles by placing the compass point on points E and F. Now points ABC create a third form that also has three curved sides, but this time they curve in rather than out. For this reason, I call it a "concave triangle." See Figure 6.

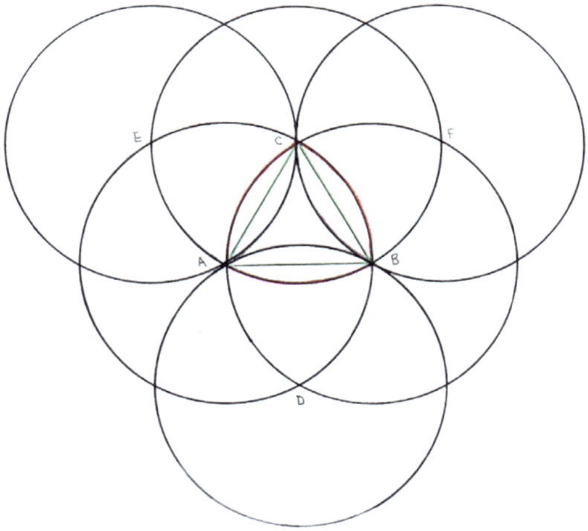


7. Having discovered these three triangular forms through the construction of Figure 6, we now draw them as three separate forms by building them up with dots or dashes as shown in Figure 7.

Clearly the central form is an equilateral triangle, but what about the other two forms? If our definition of a triangle requires three straight sides then clearly the two forms with curved sides cannot be called triangles. In spite of their convex or concave sides, however, these two forms possess a triangular quality. In that sense the two curved forms have as much "triangleness" about them as the straight-sided triangle. Although stating the obvious, it would seem that "triangleness" depends more on being "three-sided" than on having three straight sides.

8. These three variations on a triangle are ideal for showing how the contemplation of dynamic forms prepares us for meditating living archetypes:

i) Having drawn the construction of Figure 6 we now picture the construction of each of the six circles in our imagination. We picture how the circles intersect to create the three triangular forms in the middle. Then, as vividly as possible, we picture in our minds eye the three triangular forms as they appear in Figure 7.

ii) After picturing them individually, we try to picture one transforming into the other. Start with the straight-sided triangle, and then picture the three sides expanding out slightly to form the convex triangle.

iii) Then reverse the process, so that the convex triangle returns to the straight triangle. Then continue so that the three sides curve in to form the concave triangle.

iv) Conclude by imagining the concave triangle becoming the straight-sided triangle.

v) Repeat this sequence to strengthen the visual impression, but more significantly, in order to discern three distinct qualities that we experience through our feeling.

To begin with, imagining these three triangular forms changing from one to the other is another exercise in picturing moving forms rather than fixed forms. As we develop our capacity to picture one form transforming into another we not only develop greater mobility and vibrancy in our thinking, we also awaken a new capacity in our feeling.

## *From Contemplation to Meditation*

In Chapter One, we saw how our capacity to feel different qualities of warmth or coolness when looking at physical colors prepared us to call them up in our imagination. We learned to exercise "artistic feeling" as a way to contemplate non-physical or soul spiritual warmth and coolness. Beginning with physical yellow and blue, we learned to imagine and feel yellowness and blueness. When we are no longer dependent on a physical example of yellow and blue, or even an inner memory picture of them, we learn to enter into yellowness and blueness as soul spiritual qualities in their own right.

Similarly, in Chapter Two, we have exercised "artistic feeling" in order to feel the expansion of a straight triangle becoming a convex triangle, or the contraction of a straight triangle becoming a concave triangle. As we work repeatedly with the three variations on a triangle, we may discover a budding quality in the convex triangle, a crystalline quality in the straight-sided triangle, and a withering quality in the concave triangle.

To begin with we may need to behold the physical forms to discover the budding, withering and crystalline qualities. Our reliance on the outer forms will fall away as we learn to intensify our capacity to dwell within the pure soul spiritual qualities of budding, withering and crystalline. For example, we can contemplate the inner experience of "budding enthusiasm" in contrast to "withering enthusiasm". At first, we may need to recall particular outer circumstances connected to such inner budding and withering but with practice we learn to dwell within such soul qualities independent of any physical memory.

Building upon our capacity to experience soul qualities in the physical world we learn to contemplate soul qualities purely in our imagination, that is, independent of any physical manifestation. In this way we accustom ourselves to contemplating the reality of soul and spirit as a reality in its own right independent of physical reality. "Artistic feeling" is the faculty by which we are able to perceive soul spiritual qualities both within physical reality and imaginatively.

In this way "artistic feeling" also becomes the capacity that allows us to make an inner shift from contemplation to meditation. In contemplation we exercise our capacity to concentrate our attention by thinking about a spiritual content. In meditation we immerse our self within and become one with a particular soul spiritual content. To meditatively dwell within living soul and spirit archetypes such as yellowness and blueness, or budding and withering, is a modest but real step towards communing with spirit "being".

# Artistic Feeling and Three Dimensional Form Meditations

## *Spiritual Faculties*

Through the color exercises of Chapter One and the form exercises of Chapter Two, we have laid a foundation for understanding how engaging with artistic mediums can awaken and develop artistic feeling, which in turn develops spiritual organs of perception. In this chapter we will look at another dimension of artistic activity that also serves our spiritual development. In the process, we will shed light on the particular spiritual organ that is developed through artistic feeling. We will explore this experientially through another form exercise, only this time, we will do so by creating a three-dimensional form in clay.

One of the primary purposes of this exercise will be to observe more consciously our inner activity of thinking, feeling and willing as we engage in the outer activity of forming the clay. For this reason, the practical indications I give for our outer activity will be followed by observations and suggestions about what we may think, feel and will.

## *Clay Modeling Exercise*

1. We begin by creating a ball-shape in clay. For this we need a quantity of clay that fills the space between our two hands when the tips of our fingers are just touching each other. It is better to err on the side of a larger rather than a smaller lump of clay. Since I have never encountered anyone who did not know how to make a ball shape--our hands seem to know instinctively how to do this--there is no need to describe this process in more detail. While it is possible to make a clay ball with less

than full attention, it belongs to our purpose here to give our whole heart and mind to both the outer and inner activity.

2. Observing our outer activity is not difficult--it is mostly a matter of observing how our hands and fingers shape the clay. However, what it means to observe our inner activity calls for some clarification. To observe our inner activity means to observe our thinking, feeling and willing as it pertains, in this case, to making a ball shape. The first thing we are likely to observe in our thinking is that all manner of thoughts flit across our mind--some that may pertain to the ball, while others have nothing to do with it at all.

3. It is sobering to realize we are not in control of what we think as much as we might assume. Rather than dishearten, such a realization can motivate us to master our thinking. At certain times we can choose both the content and length of time we intend to think about a particular subject. In this case, we can decide to think only about the ball as we work on it. To begin with, we can set ourselves the challenge of thinking about nothing other than the ball we are making for one minute. We should not be surprised by the likelihood that we will not succeed at first. Undeterred, we simply try again for another minute. When we can give our undivided attention exclusively to the ball for one minute, we can try extending the time to two minutes, and eventually for longer periods.

4. We can help ourselves to stay focused on the ball by expanding our repertoire of things to think about a ball. A ball may be the simplest of forms,

but even a ball is composed of several elements. A ball is curved, but it is convex, not concave, and symmetrical, not asymmetrical. Conceptually, such distinctions come as no surprise but at some level we must think about such things as symmetry and convex curves if we are to achieve as perfect a ball shape as possible. As a practical matter, we need also to be sensitive to elements that do not belong to a ball, such as concavity, flatness, edges, points and asymmetry if we are to avoid them, or more likely, to transform them into the elements that do belong to a ball. For this, we need to strengthen our powers of outer observation for even the subtlest distinctions between convex, flat and concave, for example. Exact outer observation and focused thinking about the ball are the two sides of the same coin.

5. In addition to the careful outer observation of our shape and the sustained thinking about it, there are other dimensions of our inner activity we can raise into consciousness. Just as we can observe the on-going stream of our thinking, we can also observe a similar on-going stream of feelings. As all manner of thoughts can arise in us while making the ball, all manner of positive or negative feelings can flit through our heart and mind. As we can choose to make a ball in clay as an opportunity to master our thinking, similarly we can use this activity as an opportunity to master our feeling life. There is no moment in waking consciousness when feelings are not flowing through us, often below our conscious awareness and control. If we are inwardly swept along from one feeling to another, and in

that sense, at the mercy of our feelings, then we must admit we are not masters of our feelings. Just as we discovered that our thoughts can master us rather than we master our thinking, similarly, our feelings can master us rather than we master them.

6. To master our feelings is in part a matter of content—are we attending to our feelings that relate to the ball or something else. More significantly, it is also a matter of what kind of feelings we attend to. Typically our feelings manifest as like or dislike, sympathy or antipathy, pleasure or displeasure. It is a step in mastering our feeling life to control whether we feel sympathy or antipathy in any given situation. For example, we may like the cool dampness of the clay or we may dislike it. We may like the way our ball is progressing or we may be quite unhappy with it. Our feelings of sympathy or antipathy can be mild or quite intense, and very likely, they will fluctuate from moment to moment. Our feelings of sympathy/antipathy, great or small, are the most familiar form of feelings but they are not the only kind we experience.

7. Feelings of sympathy and antipathy, like and dislike, are in fact the most primitive form of feeling. We may experience a rollercoaster of feelings towards our ball—now we love it, now we hate it, up and down in varying degrees without fully realizing our feelings are related to how successful we are, for example, in making our ball less lop-sided, more symmetrical. Such a situation lends itself to our discovering another kind of feeling experience. Instead of focusing on our personal feeling of sympathy or antipathy, we can direct our atten-

tion to the particular quality of our form that we are reacting to. For this we must turn our attention to the elements of form that are present. For example, does the form have a more active quality because it is asymmetrical, or is it more at rest because it is symmetrical? Does it feel vibrant and buoyant because it is more convex or does it feel weak and withering because it is more concave? The shift from feeling like and dislike to feeling qualities of form is a subtle but significant shift to an entirely different kind of feeling experience. We move from subjective feeling to an objective feeling. This is another way to understand what Rudolf Steiner is referring when he uses the term artistic feeling. Artistic feeling can be cultivated through artistic exercises for the making of works of art, but here we are considering how the development of artistic feeling through artistic exercises prepares us for meditation.

8. As we progress in making our ball shape, as well as progress in controlling our thinking and feeling, we can decide to transform the ball into another shape. The task is not to make a new shape, but to transform the ball into a different form called a tetrahedron. Everyone knows what a ball shape looks like, but not everyone has heard of, or can picture a tetrahedron. When they do see one, most people think of a pyramid shape. This is not wrong but it is not an Egyptian pyramid. An Egyptian pyramid has four triangular surfaces converging at the peak, but it also has a square base, for a total of five surfaces. Tetra-hedron means four-sided solid and thus refers to the fact that it has only four sides, not five. We will see presently, however, that it is

not necessary to have seen one or know the name tetrahedron. in order to make one.

9. a) Before proceeding, we put our clay ball down for a moment. Without any clay in our hands, we curve them as we would to make a ball. While it is natural to curve our hand, it is possible, if less natural, to hinge our strengthened fingers and palms to create a right-angle..

b) Next, we place one hand over the other so that each hand is a flat plane and parallel to each other. While remaining parallel to each other we then adjust our hands so that the fingers of one hand are pointing away from us while the fingers of the other hand are at right angles to the first hand. Keeping our hands at right angles to each other, we now create an angle with each hand as described above--hinging our fingers at the knuckles. In this way each hand makes two flat planes at right angles to each other.

c) After going back and forth a few times between curved hands and angled hands, we place our clay ball between our hands again. At first, our hands naturally curve around the ball, but now we try squeezing it by hinging both hands at the knuckles to make right-angles, making sure that the two hands are also at right angles to each other. In this way our hands create 2 x 2 = 4 planes that correspond to the four planes of the tetrahedron.

d) In reality, our form will still be mostly curved but with a little luck we should see the first suggestion of the four planes. From this beginning we continue to develop the planes so they get larger, and eventually, flatter. Getting the four surfaces truly flat takes some time and effort and therefore cannot be rushed.

e) As central as it is to have perfectly flat surfaces, the

most important thing to focus on in the beginning is not how flat and smooth the surfaces are but to concentrate on getting the four triangular surfaces properly aligned to each other. The best way to achieve this is not through any technical aid but to work on the form from a particular view.

f) Place the emerging tetrahedron on a board or the table so that it rests on one of the four surfaces. Then look down directly from above at the top peak. It should be directly in the middle of the triangular base. Very likely it will tilt to one side or the other, in which case we can move it more to the middle. At the same time we may see that the triangular base is not equilateral, in which case we push the clay accordingly to make it so. Rotate your form to another side every minute or two, and looking down from above, adjust the relation of the peak to the equilateral triangular base as needed.

The above description should be sufficient to get started in transforming a ball shape into a tetrahedron. Further indications are not necessary because figuring out how to perfect your tetrahedron belongs to the purpose of this form exercise. The above descriptions were given in part as instructions, but more importantly they represent the thoughts we must have in mind in order to transform a ball into a tetrahedron. If any problems arise—for example, some other shape like an Egyptian pyramid—it is most likely due to some omission in our thinking so that our hands are not guided by the appropriate thoughts. Determining where something is missing and how to adjust accordingly is central to the purpose of this exercise. Once we get on track with the right conceptual orientation most people, including those who have never seen one before, are able to transform their piece so it gradually approaches the ideal form of a tetrahedron.

Let us now reflect upon the full range of our experience as we were making a ball and transforming it into a tetrahedron. This will vary with each person but something of the following can be expected:

i) *Cultivating Self-Directed Thinking*: We hold certain thoughts, and not others, that are needed to guide our hands in making a given shape. necessary to guiding our hands in making a given shape. Our thinking directs our will our will that otherwise would be chaotic and unformed.
ii) *Cultivating Self-Directed Will*: While our thinking directs our will activity, conversely, we must exercise our will to begin the forming activity of our hands. Even when the initial idea comes from someone else, our individual will must initiate the process. Furthermore, it takes inner will to hold on to the particular thoughts needed to make a ball or tetrahedron form.
iii) *Cultivating Artistic Feeling*: While we are modeling in clay, we may feel varying degrees of sympathy and antipathy towards the clay, the ball shape, changing it into a tetrahedron, and other things. When our attention and interest shifts from feelings of like/dislike to feeling the qualities of roundness and symmetry, for example, we exercise artistic feeling in developing a harmonious and whole form.
iv) *Cultivating Positivity*: At least some of the time, we may feel discouraged or disheartened by things like the slowness of our progress, or our inability to shape the form as we want it. To keep going we must overcome and transform such negative feel-

ings into positive ones. We can do this by appreciating whatever progress we have made—seeing the glass half-full rather than half-empty. Or we imagine the order and harmony of the final form so vividly that it motivates us to bring the form to completion.

v) *Cultivating Openness*: Often we get stuck because we are unable to see how to go forward, or we lose interest and are tempted to start over or make something different. When we get stuck, bored, or in that sense closed, we can open our self to the possibility that some new insight, experience or capacity has yet to reveal itself.

vi) *Cultivating Perseverance*: It takes an act of will to begin, but it also takes self-directed will to persevere, to not give up or change our form into something else. It takes inner effort or will to see what needs further work, and to develop the necessary skill to continue perfecting our form. It also requires inner will to continue perceiving our inner activity, and on that basis, to recognize and overcome any of the inner hindrances we discover in our thinking, feeling and willing.

There may well be other dimensions of our inner activity where we observe challenges and obstacles in addition to the ones mentioned above. The main thing is to begin seeing how outer challenges originate as inner challenges to our thinking, feeling and will. In summary, the making of a clay ball and transforming it into a tetrahedron provides an opportunity to cultivate:

self-directed thinking
self-directed will
artistic feeling
positivity

openness
perseverance.

Each of these attributes can be valued and cultivated for their own sake. However, in the following excerpt from his book, *Knowledge of Higher Worlds*, Rudolf Steiner shows how these six attributes develop a specific spiritual faculty that lies literally at the heart of our human potential:

*"A teacher of spiritual science who gives advice or instruction will, at the same time, always explain to those striving for higher knowledge the effects produced on body, soul and spirit, if his advice and instructions be followed." p 131*

*Now when the student begins his exercises, the lotus flowers (or chakra) become more luminous; later on they begin to revolve. When this occurs, clairvoyance begins. For these flowers (chakras) are the sense organs of the soul, and their revolutions express the fact that the clairvoyant perceives supersensibly. p 134-5*

*Now certain activities of the soul are connected with the development of these organs, and anyone devoting himself to them in a certain definite way contributes something to the development of the corresponding organs. In the sixteen-petalled lotus, eight of its sixteen petals were developed in the remote past during an earlier stage of human evolution....Man himself can now develop the remaining eight petals by means of conscious exercises...*

*The twelve-petalled lotus situated in the region of the heart is developed in a similar way. Half its petals, too, were already existent and in active use in a remote stage of human evolution...they appear of themselves and begin to revolve when the student sets to work on the other six. Here again he learns to promote this development by consciously controlling and directing certain inner activities in a special way.*

The development of this sense may be furthered in the following manner:

i) To begin with the student endeavors to regulate his sequence of thought (control of thought).
ii) An equal consistency in his actions forms the second requirement (control of actions).
iii) The third requirement is the cultivation of endurance (perseverance).
iv) The fourth requirement is forbearance (positivity) toward persons, creatures, and also circumstances.
v) The fifth requirement is impartiality toward everything that life brings (openness).
vi) The sixth requirement is the cultivation of a certain inner balance (equanimity).

*The reader will recognize in the qualities here described the six attributes which the candidate for initiation strives to acquire. The intention has been to show their connection with the spiritual organ known as the twelve-petalled lotus flower."* p 151

Rudolf Steiner, *Knowledge of Higher Worlds*

Although Rudolf Steiner does not explicitly make the connection, I believe his descriptions about developing the twelve-petalled lotus flower, or heart chakra, through cultivating the above six attributes, answers the question: What spiritual faculty is developed through artistic feeling?

Artistic feeling awakens and develops the etheric heart or heart chakra.

*"It should be remarked that artistic feeling, when coupled with a quiet introspective nature, forms the best preliminary condition for the development of spiritual faculties."*

Rudolf Steiner, *Knowledge of Higher Worlds*, p. 41-2

Building upon all we have considered, we have both a conceptual and experiential basis for seeing "artistic feeling" as belonging to the six attributes of the heart chakra. We have seen how "artistic feeling" transforms our feeling from personal sympathy and antipathy into an organ for perceiving non-physical qualities as an objective phenomenon in the world. We exercise "artistic feeling" when we perceive a qualitative imbalance—too hot, too cold etc.—in order to create a qualitative balance or harmony in a painting or sculpture, but most significantly, in our self or in some situation in the world. When Rudolf Steiner speaks of cultivating equanimity, I believe he does not imply some kind of suppressing or eradicating of feelings, but rather in plumbing the depths of our feeling life. Only in going more deeply into the realm of qualities are we truly able to cultivate inner equilibrium or equanimity as a new capacity.

"Artistic feeling" is also involved in transforming negativity into positivity. Negativity rules our mood and attitude when our feeling life is limited to feelings of like and dislike. Positivity is not simply eradicating antipathy and only feeling sympathy. Authentic positivity means we see the actual potential of a form we are creating, and more importantly, of another human being, including our self. It is through artistic feeling that we intuit the spiritual archetype of a form as much as of another person.

I submit that all six of these attributes involve artistic feeling in one way or another. Most certainly, the general capacity to observe our inner activity, to recognize when and where we are challenged by some unfree quality in our selves depends on the qualitative perception of artistic feeling. And to balance and harmonize all these qualities is to work creatively on our self as a living work of art. We are the work of art, and cultivating these six attributes is our artistic method.

I conclude this essay on artistic feeling and meditation with two passages that suggest the need to cultivate a fuller imagination of human life. It is only in the context of an expanded sense of human nature and human potential that we will come to see the full scope and potential of art. Ultimately, the human story culminates in resolving the apparent tension between realizing our full potential as individuals and our potential to build community with other individuals.

*"The enlivening of the heart chakra is a task of our present time and the near future, and represents the new stage in a modern path of self-development. The awakening and enlivening of this chakra only became possible toward the end of the nineteenth century, at the beginning of the Michaelic age—to be precise in November 1879. The enlivening or also, firstly, the awakening of the twelve-petalled chakra is the central task of our time and the focus of all efforts made on the esoteric path of schooling... The central focus of these changes is the transformation of purely logical thinking into a wholly new kind of thinking, characterized by Steiner in various different ways as: organic-living thinking; thinking which goes 'beyond logic'; 'thinking with the heart' or 'heart thinking.'"*

Florin Lowndes, *Enlivening the Chakra of the Heart*, p. 38-9

*"True human love is rooted in the spirit... Wherever such love is truly avowed and truly received, impulses will invariably be present which prepare the way for a real logic of the heart. The logic of thinking can lead to the greatest egotism. The logic of the heart is capable of gradually overcoming egotism and making all people part of an all-encompassing human community."*

Rudolf Steiner, *Macrocosm and Microcosm*, Lecture 11

# Artistic Feeling and the Etheric Heart

In a seemingly simple sentence in *Knowledge of Higher Worlds*, Rudolf Steiner outlines a path by which art and spiritual development become one and the same thing:

*"It should be remarked that artistic feeling, when coupled with a quiet introspective nature, forms the best preliminary condition for the development of spiritual faculties."*

Rudolf Steiner, *Knowledge of Higher Worlds*

I wonder how many people read this sentence and stop to ask themselves: What does Rudolf Steiner mean by artistic feeling? How does artistic feeling play a role in developing spiritual faculties? And specifically, what spiritual faculties are developed through artistic feeling?

When speaking about the artistic forms he created for the Munich Congress in 1907, Rudolf Steiner said the following:

*"A true understanding of the matter cannot be reached if observation of the forms is based solely on intellectual explanation. It is necessary to contemplate the forms with true artistic feeling..."*

Rudolf Steiner, October 1907

From these two passages we can surmise that Rudolf Steiner used the term "artistic feeling" with a specific meaning. When we look at colors, for example, it is commonplace for us to like some colors more and other colors less. As natural as it is for us to feel sympathy and antipathy for color, and much else, such feelings constitute only the most basic level of human feeling. When focused on our feelings of like and dislike of a color, we are unlikely to feel, for example, the relative warmth or coolness of the color. Instead, we are simply feeling our own unconscious reaction to such qualities.

Warmth and coolness belong to our outer experience of

the physical world, but we also experience warmth and coolness as an inner quality in ourselves and other people—as when we feel warmly or coolly towards someone.

Color appears to our sense of sight through the physical substances used to make pigments. But color itself is non-physical insofar as it embodies a non-physical quality such as inner warmth and coolness. Artistic feeling is the capacity by which we perceive and experience this non-physical dimension of the world, allowing us to distinguish soul qualities from physical qualities, on the one hand, and our personal sympathies and antipathies, on the other hand.

Artistic feeling is a capacity that artists cultivate and exercise in creating works of art, but it is equally a faculty for all human beings to cultivate in order to perceive the non-physical qualities present in all sense perceptions.

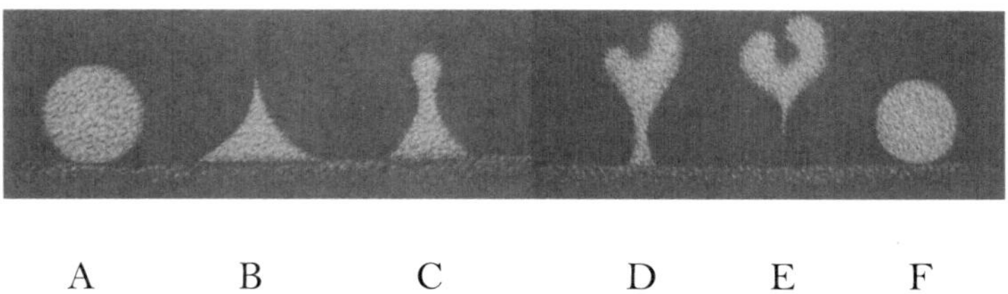


As with color, we can exercise artistic feeling in the realm of form, such as those in the above diagram. To begin with, we observe what thoughts and feelings arise in us. Are we more in our thinking, trying to figure out what they represent or mean, or possibly analyzing attributes such as their height and width? Or, are we focused on our feelings of like for some forms and dislike for other forms?

We need not eradicate such thoughts and feelings; we simply need to become conscious of what is otherwise unconscious so as to create an inner space for other thoughts and feelings to rise into consciousness. For example, we might imagine form A transforming into form B. In so doing, the forms are no longer static and separate but instead one form changes into the other form. Now that we see the forms in motion, it should come as no surprise that we feel inwardly moved by the change in form, that is, we feel the quality of one form transformed into another quality. In this case, we feel something buoyant in A becoming more weighed down and grounded in B. With the transformation of F into E, by contrast, we feel the buoyant equilibrium of F flying away into the expansive levity of E.

Artistic feeling also allows us to feel the need to balance the weighed down quality of form B with a measure of levity as in C. Similarly, through artistic feeling we feel the need to balance the flying away of form E with the grounded weight of D.

These two form exercises ABC and FED can be drawn with paper and pencil, or in a medium such as rice that allows us to literally transform one form into another. Such a sequence of forms can also be modeled in three-dimensions with clay. Such form exercises can be practiced in a sculptural training where artistic feeling is valued as essential to any creative process. Drawing and modeling such forms can also be practiced as a way to prepare our self for exercising artistic feeling in meditation.

Having carefully observed and drawn these form sequences, we can now try to picture each form and transformation in our mind's eye, that is, imaginatively. More essential than picturing the forms is the effort to imaginatively feel the gesture of each form and transformation. In this way, we develop our capacity to feel the balancing of weight with levity, or levity with weight, as a purely inner activity without reference to any outer forms.

Such inner activity provides an opportunity to strengthen our powers of concentration. It also is a form of contemplation insofar as we exercise our capacity to be inwardly mobile in our thinking, and in that sense, develop a more living thinking. Furthermore, as we dwell imaginatively in the non-physical qualities of color and form we move from contemplation to meditation. We contemplate when we imaginatively think about a non-physical content, but we meditate when we imaginatively dwell within a non-physical quality. Artistic feeling is the capacity that enables us to dwell within a soul spiritual quality. In this way, our capacity to exercise artistic feeling is the key to meditating upon a soul spiritual content.

In conclusion, we return to the question: What spiritual faculty is developed through artistic feeling?

When we take up color and form exercises, both as drawing exercises as well as content for meditation, we can expect the following challenges:

1. To control our thinking
2. To control our willing
3. To control our feeling
4. To develop positivity
5. To develop openness
6. To develop perseverance.

Anyone who aspires to cultivate what are commonly referred to as Rudolf Steiner's Six Basic or Subsidiary Exercises—as he outlines in *Knowledge of Higher Worlds* and *Occult Science*—has reason to include artistic exercises such as the ones described above as another way to develop these six qualities. We cultivate these qualities for their own sake, but Rudolf Steiner also indicates that in developing these six attributes we awaken and develop the twelve-petalled heart chakra.

With regard to the control of our feeling, Rudolf Steiner speaks of cultivating equanimity. Typically, equanimity is understood as maintaining a state of inner balance—never getting too hot or too cold, too expanded or too contracted, and so on. The reality is that we find ourselves again and again slipping into one or the other pole. What matters is our inner effort to balance one-sided qualities, not avoid them. We can do this, for example, by bringing coolness into our hotness, or levity into our weight—as form C brings levity into the weight of form B. This self-directed activity of inner balancing based on our self- perception of imbalance depends on our capacity for artistic feeling.

This suggests that the spiritual faculty awakened and developed through artistic feeling is the etheric heart or heart chakra.

The anthroposophical art impulse is founded less in any particular spiritual content or artistic style and more in the potential of each art to play a role in developing spiritual faculties in the human being. Central to the anthroposophical art impulse is the all-human significance of nurturing the seemingly humble faculty of artistic feeling. Wherever, art provides an opportunity to exercise artistic feeling, art awakens and develops the etheric heart, not only in artists but in all human beings.

*"The enlivening of the heart chakra is a task of our present time and the near future, and represents the new stage in a modern path of self-development. The awakening and enlivening of this chakra only became possible toward the end of the nineteenth century, at the beginning of the Michaelic age—to be precise in November 1879. The enlivening or also, firstly, the awakening of the twelve-petalled chakra is the central task of our time and the focus of all efforts made on the esoteric path of schooling... The central focus of these changes is the transformation of purely logical thinking into a wholly new kind of thinking, characterized by Steiner in various different ways as: organic-living thinking; thinking which goes 'beyond logic'; 'thinking with the heart' or 'heart thinking'."*

Florin Lowndes, *Enlivening the Chakra of the Heart*, p. 38-9